SPRING AND A THOUSAND YEARS
(UNABRIDGED)

Miller Williams Poetry Series
EDITED BY BILLY COLLINS

SPRING AND A THOUSAND YEARS
(UNABRIDGED)

POEMS BY

JUDY

HALEBSKY

The University of Arkansas Press
Fayetteville
2020

24 23 22 21 20   5 4 3 2 1

Designed by Liz Lester

⊗ The paper used in this publication meets the minimum
requirements of the American National Standard for
Permanence of Paper for Printed Library Materials Z39.48-1984.

Library of Congress Control Number: 2019956865

In memory of Sandor Halebsky
1930–2019

As for the spring, the dawn

—Sei Shōnagon

CONTENTS

When the University of Arkansas Press invited me to be the editor of its annual publication prize named in honor of Miller Williams—the longtime director of the press and its poetry program—I was quick to accept. Since 1988, when he published my first full-length book, *The Apple that Astonished Paris*, I have felt keenly indebted to Miller. Among the improvements to the world made by Miller before his death in January 2015 at the age of eighty-four was his dedication to finding a place for new poets on the literary stage. In 1990, this commitment became official when the first Arkansas Poetry Prize was awarded. Fittingly, upon his retirement, the prize was renamed the Miller Williams Poetry Prize.

When Miller first spotted my poetry, I was forty-six years old with only two chapbooks to my name. Not a pretty sight. Miller was the one who carried me across that critical line, where the "unpublished poets" impatiently wait, and who made me, in one stroke, a "published poet." Funny, you never hear "unpublished novelist." I suppose if you were a novelist who remained unpublished you would stop writing novels. Not the case with many poets, including me.

Miller Williams was more than my first editor. Over the years, he and I became friends, but even more importantly, before I knew him, I knew his poems. His straightforward, sometimes folksy, sometimes witty, and always trenchant poems were to me models of how poems might sound and how they could *go*. He was one of the poets who showed me that humor had a legitimate place in poetry—that a poem could be humorous without being silly or merely comical. He also showed me that a plainspoken poem did not have to be imaginatively plain or short on surprises. He was one of my literary fathers.

Miller occupied a solid position on the American literary map, though considering his extensive career and steady poetic output, it's surprising that his poems don't enjoy even more prominence. As his daughter became the well-known singer and recording artist that she is today, Miller came to be known as the father of Lucinda Williams. Miller and Lucinda even appeared on stage together several times, performing a father-daughter act of song and poetry. In 1997, Miller came to the nation's attention when Bill Clinton chose him to be the inaugural poet at his second inauguration. The poem he wrote for that day, "Of History and Hope," is a meditation on how "we have memorized America." In turning to the children of our country, he broadens a nursery rhyme question by asking "How does *our* garden grow?" Miller knew that occasional poems, especially for occasions of such importance, are notoriously difficult—some would say impossible—to write with success. But he rose to that occasion and produced a winner. His confident reading of the poem before the nation added cultural and emotional weight to the morning's ceremony and lifted Miller Williams to a new level of popularity and respect.

Miller was pleased by public recognition. What poet is immune? At home one evening, spotting a headline in a newspaper that read POET BURNS TO BE HONORED, Miller's wife Jordan remarked "They sure have your number." Of course, it was the day dedicated annually to honoring Robert Burns.

Miller's true legacy lies in his teaching and his career as a poet, which covered four decades. In that time, he produced over a dozen books of his own poetry and literary theory. His poetic voice tends to be soft-spoken but can be humorous or bitingly mordant. The poems sound like speech running to a meter. And they show a courteous, engaging awareness of the presence of a reader. Miller knew that the idea behind a good poem is to make the reader feel something, rather than to merely display the poet's emotional state, which has a habit of boiling down to one of the many forms of misery. Miller also possessed the authority of experience to produce poems that were just plain wise.

With Miller's sensibility in mind, I set out to judge the first year's contest. I was on the lookout for poems that resembled Miller's. But the more I read, the more I realized that applying such narrow criteria would be selling Miller short and not being fair to the entrants. It would make more sense to select manuscripts that Miller would enjoy reading for their own merits, not for their similarity to his own poems. That his tastes in poetry were broader than the territory of his own verse can be seen in the variety of the books he published. The list included poets as different from one another as John Ciardi and Jimmy Carter. Broadening my own field of judgment brought happy results, and I'm confident that Miller would enthusiastically approve of this year's selections, as well as those in previous years.

The poems in Jason Iwen's *Roze & Blud,* winner of the 2020 Miller Williams Poetry Prize, are split into two sections, with a change of speakers in between. First Roze Mertha speaks, then William Blud. Iwen, the poet giving this pair the powers of speech, is a distant literary cousin of Robert Browning, for both poets are interested in how the human character—soul, really—reveals itself in speech. Get someone to talk long enough and the truth about them will be known.

Roze's poems enter without knocking. Here are few of her opening lines: "They shouldn't let men as young and beautiful / as Mr. Fiedler teach high school." "I love the smell of fabric softener on the breeze." "How can a boy as dumb as Ash Reed / make someone like me horny?" "I live with my real dad in a trailer park / on a ridge above town, / and Mom's already on her third husband, over in Wisconsin now." The subtle "town / now" rhyme in that last quote along with an ability to reflect on the bedrock themes of the beauty and the brevity of life hints at a poetic maturity that emerges as we wade deeper into her poems. Roze's down-home, earthy voice arises from her life in a "shitty little beautiful / trailer park." Her world, which smells of "Old Spice and cigarettes," is part of the familiar landscape of rural American poverty where the young die of drugs, car crashes, or their own hands. Iwen dodges the inherent dangers of sentimentality and anger by giving Roze a straightforward, authentic voice. She doesn't decry her disadvantaged life; she personifies it. A friend "dropped acid in the park / and woke up on Broadway." "Whenever neighbor Angie went on a bender, I knew / because her kids weren't at the bus stop in the morning." Through the natural cadence of her talk, Roze invites us into her life without making any more or less of it than it is.

Somewhere in this procession of poems, a shift occurs and Roze's language becomes almost unintentionally poetic. She "can hear the Berlin Wall falling" in the voice of a boy rocker. She can also hear "a church bell echoing / in the ruins of a city." As she becomes more reflective, the poems turn into existential meditations on the same obsessions that drove the poems of Keats or Yeats. Here's a sample: "We could go on into the unknown / and completely forget one another / until one distant day / we smell tomato soup and tuna / and think, oh my god / that smells like something I ate / when I was in love." This group of linked poems leads to no conclusion other than Roze; s maturation. Roze stares directly into some terrible truths (she calls pain "our final companion") but her final lines contain a limited hopefulness as she imagines the dead who will "die again in us / rise again in us."

William Blud, a former boxer and an aging Vietnam veteran, has graduated from the school of hard knocks. "I've known the intimacy of the world / mostly by blows, rib by broken rib / nose by broken nose." Shrapnel is buried "like treasure inside" him. An apparent victim of PTSD, he is haunted by memories not just of war but his childhood. "I awoke to the familiar sound / of artillery in the distance / but I lay on a soft bed. / Diaphanous blue drapes / rose and settled and rose again." He accepts the diagnosis: "It is a terrible condition, I know / but I am told it is only temporary, / that only the horizon endures." He is a man leaning against a lamppost in the rain, soaking wet; a man waiting for a friend under an overpass; a man who visits children's graves in a cemetery; a creature of winter; a kind of last-man-standing who is left to elegies about his dead friends and his dead wife, Mary. He has empathy for the animal world, a fondness for walking, and enough remaining grit and a bitter sense of irony to end his elegy for Mary with "I don't need to tell you / I always hated that cat. / There, I said it again." A vein of self-pity runs through these poems, but that is true to the aim of the dramatic monologue: to reveal character, no matter what. If the path of young Roze lies ahead of her, the path of William Blud lies behind him. Full of regret and sadness, he is best left with this alert apprehension in an empty parking lot "where a fox stands in the falling snow, / and nothing else moves / but the bouquets of breath / taken from us by the breeze. / The fox watches me, and I watch it. Neither of us will move / until one of us moves."

The poems in Judy Halebsky's *Spring and a Thousand Years (Unabridged)*, finalist for the 2020 Miller Williams Poetry Prize, exist in a state of paradox, the speaker of this collection being poised between contemporary American culture and a China that is both geographically and chronologically remote. One foot is in the familiar world of bike rides to the movies and "T-back tankinis;" the other is planted in the world evoked by Chinese poetry, which speaks in the language of "moon," "nest," and "wing beats." At several points, Halebsky seeks to bridge these two realms by writing letters to Li Bai, the eighth century poet known also as Li Po. The epistolary approach underscores the sharp contrasts between the two spaces and times. The results are sometimes humorous as the poet tries to explain the oddness of American life: "They sell beer in cans . . . I know, it's amazing."

At other points Li Bai, who "wants to meet Robert Hass," and his fellow master poet Du Fu are teleported (why not?) into their future / our present, where they smoke cigarettes, ask about Charles Wright (not the one who sings "Express Yourself"), and play cards with a deck that's missing an ace. All this chronological play produces some jarring moments as when Li Bai orders a bourbon in a karaoke bar. Such moments come off as playful skits, but as a whole, this book is guided by serious intent. The environment is not ignored. Whales are disappearing. The globe's waters are rising.

Halebsky's stylistic range is on full display when she switches from pure observation (moon, water) to a kind of revved up American rap. This is how she likes her free verse: "I want it big like a cherry, a boob job in an anime film, the biceps of a trainer at Gold's Gym. Bursting, pushing on prose, veering toward some movie script with popcorn and hair salon updos and all the hours until dawns." In lesser words, she likes the unleashed energy of poetry, and in the poems gathered here, she delivers.

There seems to be no such thing as a typical poem by Angie Mazakis, whose collection *I Was Waiting to See What You Would Do First* is also a finalist for the 2020 Miller Williams Poetry Prize, mostly because this book is bursting with variations in form and sensibility. But here is a clue:

> The newspaper says,
> "Woman in Iceland
> Unknowingly Joins
> Search for Herself."
> She heard her own ·
> description and it was

a resemblance she
couldn't imagine, long
eraser strokes softening
her temples, eyes drawn too
wide. She said "No one ever
discovers me," and even when
she blew her *cover*
she was missed.

On display here are an attraction to oddities and a fondness for paradoxes, especially ones that collapse on top of each other. What follows those lines is "When I look / at a missing girl's / child photo, I don't know her, / but I feel like only / I know the nuances in her / face." Many of these poems present a provisional narrative which, by the end of the poem, is overwhelmed with asides. Mazakis tirelessly shuttles back and forth between the mind and the world, the psyche and the bus stop, creating a perfect mix of clarity and mystery. She seems to be as fascinated by the external world as she is by her internal life. Her most arresting insights occcur when she allows herself to be distracted, or better still, when she becomes the distraction, then vanishes with it under her arm. The attention demanded from the reader by these poems is exhilarating.

Shifting planes of reality and intention make up much of the imaginative play here. In a poem titled "I Miss the Friday Train and Have to Take the Monday Train," we accept the suspension or disappearance of the weekend, but other entities slide in and out of focus as well. "Once I unexpectedly saw a person I loved in my hometown, and then my hometown was no longer my hometown, just a place he was and then wasn't anymore." Another poem is presented like a movie, that is, scene by scene, but here the scenes repeat or contradict one another, and characters walk "out of the frame" and reappear as extras. Turn the page and a love affair is mixed together with the predicament of a couple stuck on Everest, running out of oxygen. There's a poem consisting only of quotes from the TV show "Hoarders." A favorite of mine titled "Aircraft Safety Information Pamphlet," begins,

The cartoon guy lifting the raft has one hand

resting on his knee like this is old hat, this
releasing the raft from the aircraft.
He's been here before.

Such helpful titles and formal patterning give the reader just enough
reality to hang on to as Mazakis takes us on a freedom ride of associa-
tions, droll reflections, and strange observations. We know where we are
going, then we don't. We are quickly moved from expectation to surprise
and back again. And to entice you, here are a few of many local delights
"We've agreed not to appear in each other's dreams" and "I make a face
like I see someone I know outside the train, but they can't see in." Finally,
in a poem titled "Illusions of Self-Motion," lies this lovely speculation on
the consequences of gravity increasing in strength: "You pull gravity in
close, / the stars compressing until Orion's cloak falls to earth." There are
no apparent limits to the imaginative reach of Angie Mazakis.

Congratulations to all three of these poets. The press is honored to
be the home for these titles for years to come.

Billy Collins

ACKNOWLEDGMENTS

I am grateful to the editors of the following journals, who published these poems (some in earlier versions): *American Poetry Review (APR)*, "Overshopping, n. /'oʊvər'ʃɑpɪŋ/"; *Adirondack Review*, "Addendum: Fifth Moon," "Days Idle, Cumulative," and "River Merchant in Blue"; *Antioch Review*, "Dear Li Bai" (published as "Dear Li Po"); *Blackbird*, "Making Shore"; *Cincinnati Review*, "Between Jenner and a Pay Phone"; *Denver Quarterly*, "Wood Carver's Manifesto"; *Harvard Review*, "In Season"; *Midwest Quarterly*, "Over the Fence"; *Michigan Quarterly Review*, "The Playoffs" and "About Last Night"; *Penumbra*, "Flight Pattern," "Bird of Prey," and "Skinny Jeans and the Known Universe"; *Poetry Flash*, "Field Exam," "Ikebana Instructions" and "Sky of Wu"; *Pretty Owl Poetry*, "O in Red"; Sixteen Rivers Press Anthology *America, We Call Your Name: Poems of Resistance and Resilience*, "Alternative Facts"; *Washington Square*, "Season Marker 1"; *WomenArts Quarterly Journal*, "Post-Season"; and *Zyzzyva*, "Tenure."

Huge thanks to Billy Collins, David Scott Cunningham and the team at University of Arkansas Press for their diligent and passionate work in making this book a reality. Thanks to the wonderful poet and editor Molly Bess Rector for her guidance and for indulging the unpaired parentheses, variations in capitalization, and the melding of prose and lyric styles of punctuation. Fellowships from the Vermont Studio Center and the Japanese Ministry of Culture and a Graves Award provided me with support and community in writing these poems. Thanks to the folks at the Bagley Wright lecture series for giving me the opportunity to articulate and envision some of the formal concepts of this work. Thanks also to Lunch Poems at the University of California, Berkeley for hosting me and buoying my journey with this book.

I'm grateful to the poets and friends who were with me in writing these poems: Barbara Tomash, Joan Baranow, Alexa Weinstein, Mizuho Ishida, Claudia Monpere, Dawn McGuire, Ann Pelletier, Ayako Takahashi, Teneal Jones, Sue & Llu, Jessie LeBaron, Susan Kelly-Dewitt,

Carol & Laverne Frith, Julia Connor, Jennifer Sweeney, Dean Rader, Rebecca Black, Margaret Lanzetta, Gina Angelone, giovanni singleton, my colleagues at Dominican, the fabulous Poets Choice, the Mojo Poets, the Community of Writers at Squaw Valley and the Sacramento Poetry Mafia. I was lucky to be able to study with Reiko Yamanaka and Steven Nelson at Hōsei University and to join the two-year seminar on *Tale of Genji*. Thanks to Shigeyoshi Hara and Hajime Yamanaka for making my time at Dokkyo University so lovely and to all the poets from Hara's seminar, Nomads, and the Lunch Poems@Dokkyo series. Thanks to my mother, my sister, Uncle George, Mike and Casey for always making a home for me. And to my new family in Davis and Petaluma. Love to my partner for making life bright and for giving me a word for every plant, tree, bird, and animal.

SPRING AND A THOUSAND YEARS
(UNABRIDGED)

Between Jenner and a Pay Phone

on the longest day of June
dusk finally falls
I cut my hair flat across my forehead

Li Bai, the shadows tonight are from street lights

I'm in the middle of a parking lot
wondering where the locals drink beer

from now on:
    only practical clothing
    only blank pages

Over the Fence

we eat dumplings with chopsticks
ride bikes to the movies in the afternoon

wild parrots fly out between buildings

I pile chipped plates and vases to throw back into the sea

when I ask Jacob, *Are we going to get married?*
he says, *If you want to*

Are we going to move?
he says, *We could*

he eats popcorn on the couch with his mouth open

in him I see the shadow of a boy who wants to be picked, to be chosen,
and it doesn't matter for what

we ride home and he points to the moon

O in Red

named in diaries, written into stories
persimmon trees are older than their traces in the fossil record

O as a connective, a river, a border

at 22, my grandfather had already fought a war
and would never again find anything as thrilling

O a type of star, a type of blood, a mark of absence

under the freeway, what I thought was a concrete mural
a pattern of long grasses
is actually a kind of fossil—a death assemblage
a snapshot of what lived together in one place at one time

O for surprise, O for lament

the man in solitary confinement is thrilled to get his picture taken
he writes to his lawyer, *Now the world knows I'm alive*

By Phone Line

by folded letter, by boat, by thread line // shaped by time or water
the way a body lies in a bed \\ the last wisteria in April

Maya says she's crazy busy // I'm on the other end of the seesaw
she's heavier \ so I never come down

\ by tin-can transmission, by splintered beam, by rolling pin //
deliberate simplicity in daily living // beauty of things worn /
weathered / shaped by time or water / glazed by ash

how to be at the edges of this crowded city \\ by stamp, by ticket
by tattoo, by sick ship, by gunfire, by alphabet

// this body as a rough draft / a plan for another life // by phone line
by boat, by folded letter/ one that could be revised and started over //

Portage

don't tell my father   that the police   drive down my street
in armor   standing on their bumpers   holding AK-47s

we march down Telegraph with signs
people come out of their houses   cheer for us as we pass

at the Berkeley Y   I hear women speaking my grandmother's language
the one she tried to pass on to my father

don't tell him   country of his sleep dream
of his overland passage

he learned physics in high school so when he got drafted
they didn't send him to be boots on the ground

raised unbridled I was   unhindered by reality   I didn't know
that luck could take or leave your life

Dad says, *At 84 I'm doing pretty good*   I nod
I forget the words sometimes he says   *that's all*

Dear Li Bai,

A million times I read your letter. I know what you mean about sadness being the easy way to go in a poem. About Americans being spoiled? I see how you might get that idea.

Trust me, a cruise ship isn't a good example. I'm glad you liked Melbourne and I'm sure the Galapagos were amazing. I'll look up the pictures on the Internet (that's a new kind of library, more on that later). The cream they put on their skin is to block the sun. They want to stay young-looking. (A tan doesn't make them less white) it's complicated.)

Let me just say. The war was a kind of storm. I sat in my kitchen. I wrote sad poems. My dear Joshua joined the army. He loved the uniform. He loved jumping out of planes. He wasn't in the helicopter that crashed. He was part of the crew sent to the wreckage. They found the pieces of bodies and cleaned them and put them in groups and sent them home. He survived. We eat at taquerias and see movies about Britain. We plan family trips to the mountains. Spoiled, yes, in many ways.

I came only with your poems. I read them the night the train left Oakland. By Portland, I was beginning to doubt the translations. I kept going. We walked the sea wall in Vancouver. My father said, *Where are we? Where are we?*

It's morning here and the middle of the night in China. I keep all your letters. I promise I won't sell them at auction. I promise no more sad poems. I'll write about the rain and these mountains and how very young I am and how writing to you is just like talking on the phone. Let's make a plan to drink and hike. We can meet at base camp. I'll bring you a rainproof coat. They sell beer in cans there. I know, it's amazing.

The Sky of Wu

It's 4 a.m., the bar is closed, and Starbucks isn't open yet, so they keep talking, Li Bai at least. Du Fu is shuffling a deck of cards that is missing the ace of spades.

Play anyway, Li Bai says

Du Fu hesitates

Li Bai wants to meet Robert Hass, but I don't know his room number. And he's got a poem due tomorrow. *How about hot chocolate?* No dice.

Li Bai wants the party to start

    (I have not been displaced by the war, discomforted maybe)

Du Fu keeps shuffling

Let's write on a joker and make that an ace, I say

They scowl (novice)

    (I write letters to Joshua in Kandahar, he sends pictures back
        in uniform in a helicopter, tan with sunglasses, smiling)

Du Fu is smoking an e-cigarette. Li Bai is laughing at him. They want to meet Charles Wright but I don't have his number.

The night is already over. There's nothing that's going to start, except the nature walk and then workshop.

We don't write the poems together, I explain, *we just talk about them*

Li Bai rolls his eyes

America, he says, *it's worse than I thought*

Slide Talk: Ghost Moon

the ramp was the size of the gallery
so Acconci in *Seedbed* could hide under it
while people walked above
hearing his breath sounds and slapping sounds
as he masturbated beneath them

my mother says art is in the details

I have not seen this with my own eyes

I'm a believer in the rotation of the earth
that these hills were once the ocean floor

when the dead come back to visit the living
I look for rocks with holes
places the river burrowed into them

Jacob brings stones and a bowl of water to the gallery
plays them like a birdcall, like a flute
we call this music
undress every night
sleep like kelp

the teacher says, *Sit still*
watch one thing

she smokes
I watch the water
so much is unforgiven
the way the water shapes us
the way we can't later become unworn

Li Bai Considers Online Dating

on a clear night and a full moon, I lie on the grass
and talk to friends far away

(note to self: before writing profile, eat cookies
then resolve to lose weight, then drink beer)

I carry little, move often
the distances between cities grow
right now I am fleeing arrest in another country
(leave this out, maybe?)

my chances of returning diminish

the mountains here are lush green, jasper green
a color that won't translate but let's try—
I sit in the lecture hall and check out the painters
I want one who quits early, who stays up late
who can lie with me in the grass
leave lines of charcoal down my thigh

I'll cross the creek with my arms raised
to keep this letter dry

Bird of Prey

Should my heart turn fickle at your expense
waves would flood the Pine Ridge hills
    —#1093 from the Kokinshū

—as in waves won't flood these hills—as in—I won't yield
    not to this current
        not to this storm

osprey: a fish hawk, a bird of prey, an overly indulgent husband

my grandmother writes to my mother: *Marriage is a business arrangement*

in class, a woman says, *It's naive to think you can decide to love someone*

an osprey nests low to the ground with eggs so easily broken

even my students know this

#42 in *Hyakunin Isshu* starts, *Writing back to a woman*
who has changed her mind

(poems so often letters)

Did we not promise, tears on our sleeves

    there are waves breaking over the hills

(sleeves like hands meaning the places we touch)

osprey: steady wing beats over shallow water

    not to this current
        not to this storm

Skinny Jeans and the Known Universe

after Ilya Kaminsky

wearing a wedding ring and a baseball cap
shouting over the music to his buddy
I almost shot myself

      2 marines drinking, 3 women in skinny jeans at the bar
      cobbles, gravel, sand, silt, mud

it takes years to learn how to read
years for rocks to be broken down
the sound of letters, syllables, words, tracing lines across the page

      [a hummingbird = a tea cup]

      [a human egg = the smallest thing visible to the naked eye]

he leans over the space between our tables
puts his arm around Jacob
leans his head on Jacob's shoulder the way I do

            [mint vine and ice in a glass]

            [tracing the line across the page]

            [we lived happily during the war]

            [mostly]

I was going to do it, he says

sounding out the letters

2 marines, back from Iraq
3 women, drinking

[forgive us]

we were eating very small pieces of cake
just slivers, really

The Engagement

Naoshima, July

I wanted   to sing on the beach   but instead
he explained the ecliptic   how planets travel
        on a flat plane   how the moon
crosses the sky   on the same line   as the sun
how   when we spin   we stretch out our arms

About Last Night

the next morning, he sent a letter tied to a twig of bush clover
this was before phone calls

*an asterisk in the text means there's a note somewhere else

her only option was to wait and care
or to wait and not care

*failure & boredom are important junctures for an artist

the letter, written in lines 5–7–5–7–7
had something in it about dawn (for parting)
and autumn (for time being against us)

Glossary

Ambient—What you hear right now, wherever you are—this requires switching from hearing to listening and waiting a minute for your attention to adjust like your eyes in the dark.

America—Permeable to water, sunlight, radio waves, river runoff, mass media, mania, conspiracy theories, thunder storms.

Bumble bee, bumble bee—I am at a desk writing to Li Bai, and I can't slow down the freeway or the airplanes or the clear-cutting.

Civil Service Exam—To pass requires writing a poem.

> **Note:** If you can do this with some density of expression and some allusions to classical poems, you can get a government job, like being a mayor or a senator (I don't know about donut shop meet-and-greets but there's a lot of visiting other officials and leaving poems on their doors when they are not at home).

Clouds—A play by Aristophanes where the moon complains that the days refuse to keep up with her (which is technically true for calendars and airplanes but useless for how we sleep bare arm to shoulder). (*See* Addendum: Fifth Moon.)

Days with snow cover—What we can count and measure.

Du Fu—(*See* yoga.)

Elsewhere—A boat dock waiting area, a radio signal, a hole straight through the earth, that cafe in Horseshoe Bay where we watch the ferries come and go.

Emissary of the Bureau of Song—This is an official title, like Secretary of State. Of course, no one wants a post with secretary in the title, even if it involves sitting at a long table beside the president. They'll want you to get coffee and they'll read all of your letters and complain that you mailed them from home.

Fall—From autumn equinox to winter solstice, an object or a person pulled by gravity without any means of resistance.

Fisherman—A recluse, tiny house dweller, living in an abandoned mill in Sebastopol, someone who decides to leave this shopping mall world.

Fossil fuels—Coal, sulfur, seamen, rigs, wells, oil, comfort, ease, quality of life.

G—As a variant of C, to distinguish voiced and voiceless. (Questions Wikipedia cannot answer: What happens when we die? Why do we fail to stay together? What would have happened that day if I hadn't crossed the causeway?) I am writing this in water with a brush on the sidewalk, letter by letter, G or C voiced and voiceless. *See* Tillie Olsen, *Silences,* <u>external link</u>. For paper link see library stacks.

Geographic distribution—Range, wingspan, shade cast by tree branches, how to count whales, bird habitat, air temperature, ice floe, polar, panda, grizzly.

> **Note:** This is a record of what is living now. In the future, it will serve as a historical record.

Haiku—Frog or leaf or two images that crash together to make a third. (Study Japanese for 5–7 years and divest from all worldly possessions.)

Hair—That scene on the steps, when she takes her vows, when she cuts the hair that sweeps past her elbows, falls over her layers of robes. Named after wisteria, *Fujitsubo,* not purple for the color but for the potent vine of March. Seeing the baby grow to look more like her lover than her husband (her husband = the emperor, her lover = the emperor's son known as the Shining Prince, the year = 998, Heian = Kyoto). We can't all be chosen.

Height—I wish you were one foot shorter so we could talk easier standing up. And so I wouldn't feel like a tiny person from a different tribe, one of grandmothers and twelve-year-olds, the undernourished, gymnasts, girl twins, snow men.

Iuno—(*See* June.)

Igloo—(*See* snow angel, stone angel, snow queen.)

Intermode—The space between leaves.

Internet—The dots you see on the back of your eyelids. Veins in your arms, the night sky, a hundred thousand seashells, the story of each grain of rice, hum of a city, a generator, a power plant. The teeth of a whale, the body of a whale, a whaling ship that brought in a hundred whales, beach glass, sandstone, vapor particles in a cloud, cars on the LA freeway on the day before Thanksgiving. Irregular verbs. Pages in a textbook about the latrines of ancient Rome. Riptide pulling swimmers out to sea. Library of Congress e-books. Skeletons in the catacombs. Rocky Mountains at ten thousand feet in new snow. The distance across the ocean from California to Sendai. Things that wash ashore.

January—This year I will trace my lineage, a female line, starting with Sei Shōnagon and moving on to Jane Austen, Virginia Woolf, Adrienne Rich (search extant texts for years lost in between). I will remember that these pages have been passed down to me, some at great risk, that value is assigned, that my mother has asked me to be brave.

June—Doing yoga every morning taught by a former-Playboy-bunny turned Beverly Hills-divorcée. After class, the women console each other about private schools and ex-husbands. Juno the goddess of Rome and marriage. June from Juno and Luno, before *J* and *L* were separate letters.

Justin Trudeau on boxing—*It's not how hard you punch that matters, it's how you can take a hit.*

Karumi—Lightness.

Keener—A derogatory term for people who show up on time, showered and sober.

Kingbird—Chaser of crows and hawks. Some are crowned with red. Others are ordinary. (I'm looking in the mirror and thinking about the woman from yoga who found a blue-eyed husband to make sure her kids would have blue eyes.)

Kite—Wax or very thin paper that flies on a string in the sky.

Language—Lost or dead, whale speech or song. When the lyrics are flat-out busted, sing these words instead: *ayiyahoo yahee ma haa ya hei nahoo nahey yo.*

Li Bai—I should tell you that Oakland is a city on the coast of California with lots of things people want to buy with paper money or lines on a page tracked by a bank. This is called abstract wealth. It means money that exists separate from bags of rice or seashells or gold. It is collected and traded for actual things but in itself is just a concept. (*See* Moneymaker.)

Localizer—A landing instrument in an airplane or a writer who translates in proximities—button-fly jeans, "Stairway to Heaven," *Beachcombers.*

Matsuo Bashō—In monk's robes in Kanto, writing to Saigyō and Li Bai, driving a four-wheeler over all that precious court poetry with his bed bugs and buckwheat and working girls.

Martin—Purple martin, sand martin, house martin. The so-called bee martin is not a martin but a kingbird.

Moneymaker—Lady butt, booty, backside.

Note: Different from honeymaker, which means a bee, not a bumblebee but a baker of sweets, a lover, a sharer of bubbly water and homebrew and jeans, a collector of shells, a man who sends me pictures of wisteria vines trying to get into the house.

Murasaki[1]—Purple. The name of a character in the story of the Shining Prince. Purple for wisteria. A name attached to the author through the character (b. 978), like calling Jane Austen (b. 1775) Elizabeth Bennet. Except Elizabeth did marry, while Murasaki and Jane did not. (Leave this space blank if no dependents.)

Note: Dear *Encyclopedia Britannica*, I was checking to see if Murasaki really didn't marry. And you say that she did. But for starters, it's the twenty-first century, why do you list her as a lady of the court first and the author of *Tale of Genji* second? Would you ever say that William Carlos Williams was a physician first and an author second? (I'll check.) And why in the world would you write that Murasaki married a man and bore *him* a son, as though the baby were a gift she would pass on, a gift she would present to him like a new platter or an award for outstanding service?

Note: William Carlos Williams (b. 1883), American poet who succeeded in making the ordinary appear extraordinary. (Source: *Encyclopedia Britannica*, Monday September 26, 2016, 7:50 a.m., ten minutes after I got out of bed, realized I should go straight to the office, and instead walked around the house naked, saying out loud, *Fuck you, work.*)

Murasaki[2]—Unforgiving of those who lack elegance, who would stumble stepping up into the hallway, who would make excuses to visit her after dark, to ask to see her unshielded, to open the blinds. She was the one to have studied, to have learned to write by eavesdropping on her brother's lessons, to not contain herself at his dim wit, to answer the questions in a whisper, to have her father lament she was not born male.

Noise—Radiator, electric lights, freeway, music as the sound between dial tone, trapped fly, door lock—if we can change from busy to still.

Normal—A red Speedo, line dancing, eating at the sink; chocolate cake, skin that heals, monologue as conversation, snow melt (we calculate normal based on the last thirty years so we can measure slow changes in the climate).

Off-grid—Unaffiliated, a township, a farm, a handwritten note, a harmonica band, hip-hop in Tokyo, folk songs in Nashville, a lemonade stand.

Open[1]—The thing about the butterflies changing colors and the leaves on the ground is that a merchant would come home in fall. Not that I need this kind of accuracy. I'm just trying to read the annotations in the text, the margins.

Open[2]—*Midrash*, notes to align the written testament with the oral transmission with how we live or how *to* live (still working on this while knitting pink cat ear hat).

Portage—To carry a canoe over land between bodies of water.

Quasi-steady state—A situation changing slowly enough that it seems constant. Marriage. The location of islands and land. A forest.

Red Pine (AKA Bill Porter)—Taking on a poet name might seem like trying too hard, but this is how it is in a language that wasn't brought in from another one, so our names became sounds rather than words.

The River Merchant's Wife: A Letter—There were no monkeys, and for sure, the wife decided on her own who she would marry.

S—For wind sound. *S* for song.

Sei Shōnagon—Witty, intense, mercurial (b. 966). This wasn't her real name; she was referred to by the rank of the men in her family. She kept a journal of lists, recording and rewriting events as a young woman in the Heian court. Which was kind of like living on campus at an Ivy League school, with everyone trying to keep up and marry well. Sometimes it was too much or they'd be discovered sleeping with the wrong person. When this happened, they could take a vow to leave the secular world. Men could move between these worlds. But once a woman cut her hair, she couldn't return. (*See* hair.)

Setback—A failure, a crash, the distance of a lemonade stand from the road.

Snow angel—The long arc of arms and legs. The first step in making an igloo, which will be warmed only by body heat. (1 body = 1 100-watt light bulb.) Make an air hole at the top. The light will pass through the ice. Our breath will melt the snow smooth.

Snow queen—Not the punk band, not the deluxe sundae, not the girl, ice pale, oblivious to her own beauty.

Speaking in vain—Talking to the wind.

The border—It's not a wall but a freeway that takes cars but not people, which is why the Temescal doesn't end at 51st but goes right up to my little house, between the gas station and the Columbus Hall and Highway 24, which is why Jacob said, *It sounds like the ocean,* and being from the ocean, I know that's not what the ocean sounds like, and more than anything, that's not the air of the ocean—the dampness, the salt night—here we have diesel and jasmine, and because I am a creature like a snail or a barnacle that can love anything, I have come to nestle into this half-plastic, half-concrete ecosystem that does not see me or name me or claim me.

Threats to tree habitat—Houses, roads, parking lots, shopping malls, air pollution (especially for conifers), agriculture (because planting a field with all the same kind of tree takes away the woodlands, the forests).

The Tropic of Cancer—The northernmost location reached by vertical rays of the sun (I don't understand this concept) (maybe because I don't want to see the earth from the sky).

Umbrella—Cloth or canvas stretched over a frame to provide shelter from the rain.

Undertow—The way Becca goes back to Alex, the way a boat lurches in the wake, that rope in my chest that can't be tapped down, a riptide, a base line, a narrow current moving seaward.

Urban canopy—Buildings, trees, the things that make up a city, the space between them.

Very cloudy sky—Defined elsewhere.

Ways to send letters—The post comes six times a day in Jane Austen's London. I swear off the vein-drip pinball thrill of email (this lasts until noon). In Li Bai's China, they tie letters to the legs of migrating geese.

Way back—The farthest-back area of a station wagon.

Win–win—A thing people say to make themselves feel that their work is not corrupt. (Profit is something for nothing. Which is why the market needs to keep expanding, making us hungry for other countries, continents, vast forests, oceans, mangroves, corals, plastic bag gyres.) Pull me from the wreck, sing me out of here, lay me near the jasmine.

Wind—Swell, wind sway, wind swoon.

Wu[1]—As a distant faraway land, written as *Goten* 呉天—呉 *go* for kingdom of Wu— 天 *ten* for heaven or sky.

Wu[2]—Historical name for Jiangsu, northern Zhejiang and Shanghai (find Chinese history professor for confirmation).

Wu[3]—as Bashō set off for his *Narrow Road* journey, he wrote, *I gambled under the slim chance of returning alive.*

Wood swallow—A songbird that looks like a swallow. Even before hearing the details, I am trying to talk her out of the divorce. There's a wreck on the freeway that I'm passing without turning my head.

Xiqu—A kind of folk song popular in Nanjing when Li Bai wrote "Song of Changgan," which would become Pound's "The River Merchant's Wife: A Letter." However crooked or misshapen, it is how we first met. Before I could say *Cho-fu-sa* or had flown over the ocean. Before the Yellow Mountains and White Cloud Temple. Before I trained my right hand to count brush strokes or drank tea out of vending machines, this is how I knew you.

Yoga—Maybe it's time I learn Chinese but already I'm less agile and can't touch my toes. Maybe Du Fu doesn't care at all about what is read into his poems years later by a city girl in America (the country) (not the continent) but kind of).

Zaa-zaa—Thrashing down on ferns and moss and rooftops. Those shallow root trees, the rain, the sweep of it, the storm.

Zinger—Of all the events that led to my decline, a white bird among a flock of crows, an entire season waiting for the detective with the shady past to kiss our hero, the worst of it, the best.

Zoom—To get up close without losing focus.

Zumba—A kind of dance, an erotic gym class, associated with monogamy, middle age, and stretch pants. Related to dance clubs, where the chances of going home with a stranger are dramatically higher. This requires dance pants, similar to stretch pants but with one pocket for ID and cash. Don't bring your phone, especially if it's the Press Club (the bar, not the nonprofit) because they'll dial every number in your contact list. Whoever answers will suspect you were passed out drunk. Trying to explain will make it worse. The ex-boyfriend will say, *The Press Club? Is that the International Press Club?* He will be thrilled.

Z.cookie—Writing the word cookie with a Z before it.

> **Note:** Li Bai: *It's too much. This whole freeway, art murmur, airplane, avocado toast thing.* Du Fu: *I can't sleep one more night with central heat.*

Zule, Zuppa, Zuz, Zythum—I knew it would be a hard ending.

> **Note:** No more vegan donuts, no more craft beer. Now, I will become the girl poet packing tuna fish sandwiches in wax paper and waving from the Amtrak platform.

Li Bai: *I'm used to traveling alone.*

Me: *I know.*

River Merchant in Blue

of course I'm expecting you now
the butterflies are yellow with August
and you've sold everything you possibly could
between Gilroy and Weed

blue plum—a kind of apricot
in the damp heat of this summer night, wherever you are

blue for pale
blue for livid and leaden and bruised

know that I chose you as my spouse
you were never my king or my lord

blue for loyalty
blue for distant and unknown

a river merchant's wife—
would I rather have married a farmer?
one who would walk up behind me
put his dirt hands on my waist
one who would know
blue is for young and fresh and green

rather than what we choose
I think sometimes love is what we can't escape

—In Season, 1

most of the Milky Way is dark matter
so Jacob brings home tulips

Marvin Bell is writing poems as a dead man
maybe that's a good approach

a snail across the sidewalk
a dead bird in the surf

all the generations before me laid to the dirt

Jacob wants me to not notice
the stress on *could*
in

                we *could* have kids
          unresolved stars   unpaired particles

the galaxy is moving at 630 km/hour

he's hoping it's too late

Henry Moore, the sculptor, instructs his students,*
Roll it downhill
any piece that falls off
leave it behind

---

* as told to me by Aunt Nina and not checked or verified in any way other than
seeing the rounded stone-carved nudes and imagining them rolling downhill

Obscure, adj. or n. /əbˈskjʊ(ə)r/

how fast is the water rising?

Don't worry, he says, *the earth will be fine*

cloud wake, cloud bank, cloud mine

On a geologic scale, we are one of many mass extinctions

unenlightened, benighted, frequently in darkness

we don't see the rain cloud because it's falling

Boy Child

Instructions: at the first full moon after the New Year, make a seven-grain porridge (like Red River cereal). This wards off evil. Take a stick from the fire that was used to cook the porridge. Find one that was not burned. Strike it to my thigh. This will bring a boy child.

Or, we can see Dr. Rosen at the fertility clinic. I'll tell him about my dissertation, my low levels of vitamin D. He'll tell me that my ovaries are still young. This is a sales pitch.

he'll say at 40, we take the most aggressive approach

Jacob doesn't want extremes*

where does that leave us?

(how to read a book in translation:
          two bookmarks: one for the pages, one for the notes)

*a-wa-re: a feeling that comes from understanding the world as transient

Letter From America

Do you want stamps? I ask,
Or you could use my computer?
(Du Fu wrinkles his brow)

he writes to a handful of mountain mystics
three men with distant government posts
his wife, his brother, and two immortals

he asks, *When might we hear back?*

      Could take a while, I say

Next season maybe, when the birds come?

      Did you give them your address?

Yes, Du Fu says,
I wrote: Oakland, by the gas station
I wrote: Tahoe, near the diner
will that work?

      Are they on Facebook?

(Du Fu looks at me like I'm trying to sell him
a set of encyclopedias)

      Are they online? I say, to clarify

They are everywhere, he says

Making Shore

when they talk of those who are here only in spirit
they are speaking of my father

he is in Vancouver tonight and not at La Peña
cheering the release of Fernando González from prison

barrel hitch, timber hitch, *blood knot to mend a broken line*

the Cuban Five are free and back in Havana
my father is with them
in his seafaring apartment
where he comes in and out with brine
and a rusted anchor
no one will cut the rigging

when a stranger comes to the door, I don't answer
it's either a neighbor or a church lady
come to tell me that I can believe in science
and still be a Seventh-day Adventist

opiate of the masses—cool my veins, numb my heart
lift me from here—alpine butterfly
bowline, water knot, clove hitch

I carry bags home from the store
sit out on the porch
listen to his voice on the answering machine

he says, *You are never home*

Days Idle, Cumulative

I am on strike today with Union Local 124. This poem will have no
images, no subtle observations, no tattooed girls on bicycles. The gray
in my lover's beard is not a sign. I won't have a poem about how my
light is spent or what I might have done with that Volvo key I found on
the beach or how I sent him to the store so I could have a few moments
to lay out the demands of this work stoppage:

(1) I want all new language, I want the words hosed off and scrubbed
clean. I want to come back tomorrow and see them gleaming and
single and unattached, willing to hook up with any word that has at
least two vowels.

(2) I need a raise. I'm losing lawn share to the rising line, the vocal fry,
the volta and that endless prose-style enjambment.

(3) Don't confuse me with a haiku poet. I am firmly here in free verse.
I want it big like a cherry Slurpee, a boob job in an anime film, the
biceps of a trainer at Gold's gym. Bursting, pushing on prose, veering
toward a movie script with popcorn and hair-salon updos and all the
hours until dawn.

Okay, maybe it's possible I'm in league with haiku. A little in the pink,
colluding, organizing, making pamphlets. It's just that I have to cut so
many lines. Can we compromise? You agree to take the mediocre and
push them up to pretty good. I promise I'll keep a few more words.
Shine them in my rock tumbler. Put them on the clothesline so they
can dry out and let go of whatever dark bar they walked in from. (This
is called bargaining and there's usually a crossroads and a devil. Usually
there's something to lose.) Bashō said to live like a house on fire (that's
not an image, I'm still on strike) (it's an idiom meaning we live close
to death).

Li Bai Is Living in a Share House in the Temescal

I.

Converse sneakers, blue jeans, long hair tied back,
we meet in the morning to eat donuts.

At karaoke, I ask him, *What's your song?*

He says, *meta sequoia, dawn redwood*—let that be me
(rubber tires and freeways notwithstanding)
the one that survived only in monasteries
to be brought back,
     What are the chances?
        and rooted here.

II.

They don't have Nina Simone at karaoke. Or Joni Mitchell or Etta James. Li Bai orders bourbon. They serve him lime soda and French fries.

Correction: it's the gingko tree in the monasteries, not dawn redwood.

Extinction: in Oregon, they saw the eyelash pine needles in fossils and found none living in places they knew.

Dawn redwood: living in stands in the forests of Hubei.

Du Fu is sleeping with headphones and an eye mask. He says, *What are you going to write poems about? There's a war on.*

It's not a war, I explain, *just police and protesters.*

Li Bai makes a cardboard sign. It says *Ocean Ocean.*

Ikebana Instructions

—don't confuse self-satisfaction with freedom

—arrange the flowers to reflect an inner world

—we become what we cultivate

      a pressed yellow leaf falls out of my journal
I lie on the floor near the heater

where is the rain that is not falling here?

where is Jacob, who can trace the water lines
of the Bay in thousand-year increments?

my mother wants me to call her with the results

what shall I say?

the work of my life has been to arrange flowers
cut at the stem

Poem

to live as bright as wild as close to the fire as possible

[repeat for 14 lines]

Post-Season

In my first year of marriage I've learned about basketball and the
three-point line (different from iambic pentameter). I've ignored
monologues and direct instructions from my sister-in-law (risky, but
I had to start somewhere). We dug a hole for a persimmon tree that
now has branches and the first starts of fruit (this is not a metaphor).
I've gone to the doctor, I've calculated the odds. I've had unfurled,
untied, sea creature sex. I've learned how to walk in and out of sleep.
How to listen unmoored to conspiracy theories and can't-fail business
plans, how to drink coffee in bed in the dark (call this dawn). How to
mix chicory with angelica root, grind mint with pestle and mortar.
I've gone to bed angry—just once—in the coma of back roads (leave
this unmarked). The game is close and we're behind. A crowd on the
sidewalk is watching through the window. I'm not a sports fan but I'm
holding my breath (caesura) for the chance that we'll win.

Field Exam

State Board of Poets

Section A: Self-Identification

Hoarder, known in the field as a *nester* (check all that apply)
_____ collections of index cards, beach glass, astrological charts
_____ guides to wildflowers, native plants, old-growth trees,
     all volumes of *Clear Your Clutter with Feng-Shui*
_____ three or more boxes of debris marked: *notes for poems*

Drifter
_____ sleeping in a car, tent, or beneath a freeway underpass (required)*

    *exception if poet lives in the garage or summer cabin of wealthy
    friends (if these are family members or in-law connections, fill out
    Privilege of Birth paperwork)

    (note: drifters living out of a car but with a storage unit can write
    the *nesters* section of exam as applicable)

Romantic
_____ things are worse now / were better then (applicants who have
    sought treatment for nostalgia either through Zen training or
    moving apartments are considered to be in recovery)
_____ disdain for all kinds of feedback (makeovers, renovations,
    critiques, the process of discarding)
_____ clairvoyant
_____ party to infidelity (for open relationships, see Deal Maker
    or Drifter)

Deal Maker

_____ trained in law school to memorize and carry (not just to repeat
   back, but to carry) (trained into the body to carry) (this will be
   hard to undo)

Failure

_____ (all kinds eligible)

Section B: The Elevated Heart*

Li Bai is furious that this is even on the exam. He says, *Impossible.*
He says even the most profit-seeking, competitive, snide, selfish
heart can crack, can soften.

Du Fu suggests that applicants write an ode to loneliness every day
and then we average the results. (This proposal is on the agenda for
the next meeting.)

To elevate the heart means to cultivate attention. *In a flash of lightning,*
Bashō explained, *be ready.*

[I would go on but I kind of hate poems about poems] [since this isn't
a poem, it's an exam, and I hope you pass, I hope I pass, I hope we can
all be healed, and my father, for a moment, from the haze, would nod,
would glow, because we are trying to write a poem which will mend
the wreckage he lived through]

Grace Paley wants us to give a license to anyone who applies.
So do I, and so does my father. It's not a quorum, but we are not
counting.

Donald Hall says, *As long as they come to class and try.*

Du Fu says, *Put grade inflation on the next agenda.*

Donald Hall says, *Put no assigned grades on the next agenda.*

Grace Paley waves. She keeps waving.

*Optional Secondary Certification in Confessional Poetry. (Applicants identifying as male may choose to write the *universal themes* exam instead.)

Section C: Craft

Check all that apply:

_____ vanity
_____ debauchery
_____ frivolity
_____ optimism
_____ wildness

(*Always* and *never* are worth two points each.)

No sonnets, no trochees, no counting meter or foot. This is a living craft, which requires passage along a cliff edge, the threat of falling into blue screens and housing tracts, sitcom amphetamines, the risk of burying oneself alive.

This aligns with state standards.

Applicants who score 80 or above receive certification. Remember, we are writing with the living and the dead (see rubric). With my father and Grace Paley and all the workers who believed things would get better but didn't see it in their lifetimes. What is hidden floats, what is buried rises.

Poll Numbers in Oakland, 2016

it wasn't until the army knew they were defeated
that cities fell without bloodshed

a year ago Su Tung-P'o walked from Chanchiang to here
(to be clear, he walked from the Sung Dynasty to the Temescal)

of crossing the mountains, he wrote, *Fine rain*
on plum flowers nearly broke my spirit

(insert coin for poem to continue)

(in America, you can buy anything)

diary of love songs, advice on how to sleep through the night
pebbles from New Brunswick, Kamakura, Stinson Beach

my father doesn't remember which side of the border we're on
he doesn't believe the system can be reformed

(workshop feedback: this poem is a complete failure)

Havana, 1959, in the middle of his speech, Fidel stops
lifts his eyes across the stage, *Voy bien, Camilo?*
Camilo nods, *Vas bien, Fidel*

what's behind door #3?

Fine rain on plum flowers nearly broke my spirit

—In Season, 2

one room for sleeping, one for a garden window, one for plum trees
broken in the wind, for branches collected in a jar

I pay cash for Chinese medicine—for a balance of all things

allergy tests can't screen for toxins, plastics, or paint fumes

so they look
                        for ragweed, bee pollen, nightshade

        canary   canary

sleep with our feet pointing south

drink a broth of the forest floor

after a field burns, what grows back?
fireweed, rosebay willow, poison oak

The Playoffs

I'm at the Red Sea because the King Fish is full of twenty-somethings
in baseball caps. But the King Fish is, as my grandfather would say,
coeducational.

he would say, *It's not how hard you punch that matters*

> a spell cast by a woman, we call this *glamour*

> a woman alone, *trouble*

They offer me a seat at their table and when Curry, our baby-faced star,
misses a shot one guy yells *shit* and catches my eye, wishing that he
hadn't sworn or that I wasn't there to hear him.

I look down

What matters is how you can take a hit

When Sei passed ink pages through the Heian court, they weren't sheets
they were scrolls, women in waiting (for days and years) writing as an
extension of the body (the paper, the handwriting, the scent) hidden
in carts, behind screens in rooms named by the flowers out front.

a lover visits after nightfall, leaves at first light
(this has not changed in a thousand years)

the women composed poems as courtship, as a mark of beauty, as a
way of falling in love

I'm 42 in April, the blossoms now are pale on the ground

they had to be good at writing, but they also had to pretend
that they didn't know the rules

How to duck, how to fall, how to walk into the Red Sea

that they couldn't trace a running script or recite Li Bai by heart

that they hadn't spent secret hours reading the books
so carefully kept from them

Jacob's Wood Carving Manifesto

when water evaporates off our skin it takes away the heat

a wheat farmer can lose a whole year's crop in one hail storm

the marshal at the door asks me to come to the morgue

the wood carver says he doesn't want to be known

for always making rolling pins

by the kitchen window, watching the storm

he says, *You have to get ideas, good or bad, out of your head*

no pattern other than the grain of the wood

Li Bai Interviews for a Job at Green Gulch Zen Center

I.

No ragged beard. No wild gray hair. No ink-stained pants. In that
Macy's suit you don't look anything like the poet I know. It's just that
we each need to find some way to trade part of ourselves. (I'm trying
to not believe this) (unless you have a rich uncle or can claim a family
connection to the Kardashians, which might have worked for you in
Changgan but at Market and Geary, it's doubtful.)*

The job is to give talks and minister to those fighting death with white
dust and capsules. Sidebar: Medicine and employment both have side
effects (a seesaw, the spread of a blue heron's wings, walking the length
of a canoe). Sidebar: You really aren't the best fit for this job. There's no
drinking. And half the people in Marin are nuts. But I guess you could
talk about Mahayana and Daoism and how the two came together. It's
just that now is way after Chan Buddhism was brought to California
and way, way after it was brought to Japan. But I think they'll like the
wild parties and the legend of your death. Don't correct the story.
They like it this way: leaning out over the side of a boat, trying to
catch the moon.

*Instructions on how to dress for a job interview, for a position that might
ruin your life, are included, because I have tried this and failed [1](to get a
job) [2](to escape ruin).

II.

Question: Do you have experience working at a retreat center?

Answer: Hiding out while rebel forces stage a rebellion. That's a kind of retreat. Waiting for news of where the troops are moving. Coming up dandelion and thistle in Oakland, carrying not even the seeds from the garden in Loyang. There are four kinds of poems. Each one has a category. Partings, visiting a friend, celebrating the host, and miscellaneous—that's where I build my tree fort, that's where I go to the lookout, above the branches, open the shutter, lean my elbow into the August air, from mosquitoes to fireflies, from rope ladder to landing. I'll sleep anywhere, if not a stone roof then a tarp, a lean-to of branches, a dirt floor, a canvas bag layered with wax. This is my training for the monastery. This and breaking my vows. I've done that too.

Overshopping, n. /ˈoʊvərˈʃɑpɪŋ/

a kind of vertigo, a drug, an addiction

a leisure activity, a diet technique, love or substitute thereof

origin: America. (*See* glossary)

related to: ecstasy, art making, beauty pageants, hunting

available in: spa blue, lapis blue, cobalt, capri, cerulean

something is not an addiction unless it has a negative impact on your life

(raw materials/ sweat labor/ freight)

[to be most effective, the costs must remain hidden]

the binding of one person to another

servant/ adherent/ disciple

the state of being so bound

Credit Counseling: Transcript

him: what is this, Chinese medicine? [$300 a month]

me: the herbs come from the mountains near Shanghai

[he crosses out that line on the chart]

him: poetry? [$100 a month]

me: yeah

him: let's get that down to zero

him: what do you do on weekends?

me: take naps, go to the movies

[he crosses out movies]

me: but I don't have a TV

him: you can read books

------ end of transcript ------

Ale and Ginger

Water doesn't run through stones but pipes into houses. There's neither frost nor snow, and so few green patches I can't even wet my lips with dew. They think drinking ale in the morning is a sickness. No matter the weather, they serve it cold.

For maladies of inner strength, they have one-on-one treatment in chairs in rooms called talk therapy. They've got tiny pills and this way of bleeding blood back into the body. There's no dispelling demons unless you go across town to a singing temple where I hear they can take the devil out of you. As for talk therapy, it doesn't seem to do anything at all.

—extant part of Du Fu's letters from America

—In Season, 3

the moms of Marin come to swim at the pool
they wear visors and T-back tankinis
all around them: magnolia, wild iris
        allopathic medicine—
                the mind as separate
            from the body
cherry blossoms fall as soon as they bloom

they say I need to try another doctor
they ask me, *What else can be done?*

(we're only allowed one season marker per poem
so here you must choose:
cherry
or magnolia
or iris))

_____

I choose Janis Bell's grammar book—that I am reading so I can use
commas but it keeps giving me other instructions

resin cones split in the heat, this is what they have planned for

the swimmers are very skinny and very blond

acres burn by lightning or spark

so in the next rain a root tendril will rise through the ash

Moon Dog

when Yutaka tries to get out of going to karaoke, I tell him
Don't say no to me, I already lost the election

we're in the shrine room of Sainen-ji for haiku group
there's a machine for lighting incense
we take a break when someone comes in to pray

Yutaka asks me about my family name
I say *Russia, Ellis Island, the Bronx*

he says, *That's tough*
I say *No, it's nothing, it's not* a thing
what I mean is, it wasn't hard *for me*

7 hours, 18 beers, 3 bottles of Chinese liquor, multiple rounds of
"I Left My Heart in San Francisco," clams in spicy sauce, eggs in sweet sauce
Yutaka smokes a pipe, the monk smokes cigarettes

these are your instructions:
    calligraphy is from the body
    vacate the mind
    choose a name like Moon Dog or Radio or Lucky Pig
    (these are already taken, find another one)

across the table, a guy is passed out
his head resting against the wall

Yutaka teases me, *You just talk and talk and talk*
Kenji whispers to him, *Americans don't listen*

we wave goodbye in the rain

Monks drink beer—it's a family lineage system, not a calling
what matters is training your voice to sing the prayers

She Makes a List of *Things That Cannot Be Compared*

after Sei Shōnagon

a pear tree versus a watermelon
       a stray dog versus a tombstone

we walk past a dairy farm
the smell lingering with us as we climb

it's a two-hour loop, so Allison starts, *It was a storm of a spring*
her husband left, the house burned down, her father died
we're not even to the lookout yet

last weekend, she took a bus to New Hampshire for the funeral
the man beside her without a bag or a change of clothes

he told her the worst part of being in prison was missing the birthdays
the near-death days of his family members

             a palm reader versus a blood test
             laughter versus the same person's rage

we walk in the July dusk, flies tangling in our hair

he told her prison didn't make him a better person

he told her his father was a good man

                          a bird and a dinosaur
a bicycle versus a skyscraper, burial or cremation

Allison says it was lucky she couldn't get a car
even though the bus was two hours late

and she missed spreading her father's ashes

a lantern and a rowboat, fresh water and salt water

she says, *I was supposed to meet this guy*

a paper airplane versus a crane

My father sent him

Pacific Slope Death Poem

blue fin whale—endangered
sperm whale—endangered
humpback whale—endangered

bury my hands in the sand

Physical Description

in the last weeks of Bashō's life
students asked, *Which poem is your death poem?*
he said, *From now on, all poems are my death poem*

Status

the blossoms are out across the street
Mikey, on the other coast, is making a snow fort
Mom gained five pounds in Florida
she explains, *A total disaster*

Color

beluga whale, ghost-white like snow—endangered

Breeding

mating is complex and frequently involves three or more whales

[this poem may be reprinted for educational and scientific purposes]

they mate in the lagoons of Baja, Mexico

night jasmine is out all over the city

      bury my hands in the sand

nipples, chin, shoulders

bury me in the sand

Migration

      leaves are out now on the plum tree
      deep-shadow red
      branches up to phone lines
      wisps of clouds
      blue winter sky

Bibliography

      beer is a symbol for summer
      the moon a symbol for fall

Acknowledgments

      From now on, all poems are my death poem

Tenure

my dear Li Bai, I'm writing to you from Pizzaolo in the Temescal
where the admission is one laptop computer and a hard-boiled egg

I have the papers for my station
it's a minor court, but nonetheless—
they gave me an office key

I paid in both words and silences

I ate a dozen donuts with Allison
who doesn't believe in diet culture

spent dawn in an attic room with Tita
who doesn't believe in monogamy

what else to not believe in?

language reflects the prejudices of the society in which it evolved

birds reflect the habitat, the climate of more than a hundred thousand years

I have traveled this path with a certain kind of loneliness
or this path has not allowed me to escape the loneliness
that falls on each of us

Flight Pattern

I put my suitcase down
see the robins outside
on the window, I notice
the waxy imprint of tail feathers
faint outline of the arc of a wing

rose robins sing
as if classically trained, as if they are drunk or in a hurry
desperately and beautifully
my dad beaming that I've come to see him

I can't remember a single thing, he says

in firethorn bushes
males sing a whisper song
to mark territory, to sigh defeat
I tape squares of colored paper to the glass

he sleeps on the couch
I sleep in the bed
each morning it's the same
How does the stove work? Where am I?
What is that sound?
a bird hitting the window

songbirds navigate by the stars
but when it's foggy
when the clouds are low
they fly into the lights
that shine in dark windows

Alternative Facts

(A heavy drinker vs. an alcoholic) (floodgate vs. rainfall) (non-non-fiction) (read: it's messy) (read: we must try) (read: colonial power involves putting people into categories) (American, red blood or blue blood—this depends on the air and if the blood has left my body) (I should have finished this poem before the election) *tyranny does not begin in violence, it begins with the first act of collaboration.* I was wondering what I would do with my life. Now I see I will be filling sandbags for rising water. I will be trying to reach Dianne Feinstein on the phone. I will make myself a place of safe harbor. people without papers, people who carry scientific knowledge, people who pray. I will start before they come for me. I have no tattoos. I have not spent a night in jail. I have two passports, three bank accounts, my name on a marriage license, a house deed, dental records, blood type, insurance card, driver's license. I will be hard to erase. But not impossible.

Dear Red Pine,

my translator, my carrier of letters, my pulse link, IV feed, my dealer
I've been with our tender Wei at the East Grove doorway
looking into the house, across the bare floor

time has moved on but her traces remain (as the years since he left)
(as his wife taken by unnamed disease)

clause: I read the footnote

clause: if I could give my written name a privilege that my body doesn't have
I would name myself in lineage with the redwoods, the evergreens
with dogwoods in April, with snow geese and sparrows
Tom Thompson's northern pine—gnarled and bent by the wind

(remember this)

personality type: unhindered by reality

clause: lines across the page, a bank loan, a mortgage, a debt
a promise, a theft, a defeat

clause: hold nothing

clause: not the branches, but the wind

I think of you, my dear Red Pine, on the coast of Washington, woodstove
burning writing couplets out by hand

if it's different from this, if you are hungry or wish for another life
please, don't let me know

How to Make Music

following instructions from composer Pauline Oliveros

Dad needs someone to get groceries, to put food in the fridge, to warm it up, to tell him what day it is and explain why that kid David Noodleman changed his name

    * * *

it takes practice to listen, start now

daughter of airplanes and highways
       daughter of car keys and handbags

                  (this isn't about how long the song lasts
             it's about whether or not you can get there—the singing)

the rain is falling in sheets now   on windshields and flower pots

          the music ends by unspoken consensus

    * * *

this will be a new measure of time
       people are walking with newspapers over their heads
       how long for the Style section to disintegrate

    * * *

I lie sleepless through the night, I fail those I love
lay my head on his chest
          unveiled, unarmed

the music ends by unspoken consensus

I know he is leaving this world

       clouds   not noticing me at all
     move over the far hills

Appendix: Lost Sections of the *Pillow Book**

[these sections were found at the Bureau of Song by an appropriately depressed graduate student looking for her stash of pretzel sticks and chocolate-covered almonds**]

[57] Potions

sweet peas, dahlias, camellias

whatever I bring, he says, *That's my favorite*

rose water, a Moosehead Red label from 1992, buck-a-suck
string (don't ask)

the good news is that the cancer is not in his bones

it's the weight that can tell the ripeness of a pomegranate
not the size

two girls in sandals are moving pennies back and forth
across the table for luck

cheerfully, I say, *That is good news*

[62] Spells and Incantations

a gun-shy lover is worth his weight

a gun-shy lover pairs well with the untamed

what woman, her kind, have I been?

restless, unsettled, running out into the night
star-shaped hands, winged arms
sweet gum, black gum, hazel pine

green once with August
over rooftops and hills
by November, bright red
branches, ablaze

he waits for fate to cross his path
in the roots, in the piles of leaves

a gun-shy lover pairs well with fire
if he is water
if he can't burn

[64] *yo* = night = world

[why do you hasten thus to relinquish this night]

(quote of unknown origin)

most likely the word night
was also the word for night

why are you giving up?

to give back, to hand over, to untouch

[to relinquish this world, why do you hasten thus]

* these claims have yet to be verified by experts in the field

** from the stairwell window
bright red maple leaves
I go up and down
office work, office work
ink on my hands
leaves on the ground

Addendum: Fifth Moon

Bashō crossed the mountains of Yamagata, counting days in rain,
in sake, in some slingshot between the sun and the moon (I'm
not worried about when to plant or wear white pants or when the
dogwood branches will cover the window). Rows of English majors
are crossing the stage. The start of spring is exactly halfway between
the winter solstice and spring equinox (this has something to do with
the longest night and the shortest day) but I don't want to break any
spells, not this early in the poem, at least. When the lunar and solar
calendars got too far apart, they would add another month, say after
May but also called May with another character to note an extension
or side door, like an attic or a trunk, an extra gate for when the main
city gate is closed. It's messy. A language half-based on the fields, the
harvest, the seasons, and half-built for the tax system, with categories
and rules that we only half-fit into. The parts that don't fit are phantom
limbs that ache and call to us (remember, we can move a heart from
one body to another) (we can send messages through the air, we have
glasses to see in the night. fusion. radioactive isotopes. carbon dating).
Even these words are thousands of years old (from the Germanic
tribes, Sardis, the Lower East Side). There will be another dictionary,
traced out of ash, that aligns the day with the night. The new moon
with the harvest. The night sky with the eclipse. Concrete streets
with tires, a hydro river dam, legions of kung fu seven-year-olds with
analog synthesizers, a ukulele revival, and a phone that can name
constellations of stars (this isn't the end of the poem—even though
we've gotten totally off track and might spend the next two years
drinking vodka in the Russian space station). I'll look for one later,
which might be an end or a side gate, a way to leave the poem just after
dusk when the main gate is locked and the guards are sleeping.

NOTES

Some of these poems are informed by the literary works that influenced Matsuo Bashō (1644–1694) in his haiku and poetry journal form. This includes Japanese women's writing from the Heian era, such as the *Tale of Genji* by Murasaki Shikibu (978–1014) and the *Pillow Book* by Sei Shōnagon (966–1025). Hiroaki Sato's highly annotated translation of Bashō's *Narrow Road* highlights the many intertextual references in Bashō's work which led me to read the Chinese Tang dynasty poets Li Bai (also known as Li Po, 701–762) and Du Fu (712–770).

The epigraph to "Bird of Prey" is adapted from Sato's translation of poem number 1093 in the *Kokinshū*, a Japanese poetry anthology compiled in 905. The poem also references an untitled poem by Kiyohara no Motosuke (908–990).

"Skinny Jeans and the Known Universe" is inspired by Ilya Kaminsky's poem, "We Lived Happily During the War."

"Glossary" takes from many different sources, including the American Metrological Society's *Glossary of Meteorology* and the *Oxford English Dictionary*.

"Glossary" and "River Merchant in Blue" allude to Ezra Pound's poem "The River Merchant's Wife: A Letter," which is a translation of the Li Bai poem "Song of Changgan." Scholars have written on the many ways that Pound's translation departs from Li Bai's original.

In "Glossary" the external link goes to the Poetry Foundation webpage on Grace Paley, found at https://www.poetryfoundation.org/poets/grace-paley#about

"Poll Numbers in Oakland" quotes from Su Tung-P'o's poem "Ten Days of Spring Cold Kept Me Indoors" (1081), translated by Burton Watson.

"Alternative Facts" quotes from Evan Osnos's article "When Tyranny Takes Hold," published in the December 19 and 26, 2016 issue of the *New Yorker*.

"Dear Red Pine" alludes to a poem by Wei Ying-wu (737–791) titled "Heartbreak at Our Old Dwelling at Tungte Hermitage" and translated by Red Pine.

The title of the poem "Sky of Wu" comes from a passage in Bashō's "Narrow Road" translated by Sato, "I casually thought of making a pilgrimage over a long road to Ōshū and, even while realizing that I could end up regretting my hair turning white under the sky of Wu, I gambled on the slim, uncertain chance of returning alive from a place of which I had heard but hadn't seen with my own eyes."